Grans and Grandads

Hawys Morgan

Illustrated by Alex Hoskins

Schofield&Sims

Luca and his grandpa make bread together.
Luca eats every crumb!

How to make bread

1. Add water to bread mix in a bowl.

2. Stretch and knead it.

3. Wrap the bowl with a cloth. Let it rise somewhere toasty, like a sunny windowsill.

4. Use a knife to make a design on the top.

5. Bake it until it's a golden brown.

Farzeen helps her grandad at work.
He's a plumber.

Oliver helps his granny at work, too.
She's a farmer.

Amber's dad is on night shift. Her grandma braids her hair before bedtime.

How to braid hair

1. Use a comb to get rid of any knots.

2. Use your thumbs and index fingers to twist the hair together.

3. Wrap hair bands around the braids. It looks nice!

Yanlin calls her grandfather in Hong Kong. They exercise together.

Did you know?
When it's lunchtime in London, it's bedtime in Hong Kong!

Victor's grandparents live in Poland. They love gardening.

They write letters to Victor and send him photos of their beautiful garden.

shoe flowerpot

In the holidays, Victor visits his Polish family.

garden gnome

Did you know?
One Polish town is known for its gnomes!

Connor and his nan knit bright designs together.

They wrap them around things in town. This is called yarn bombing.

How to yarn bomb a tree

1. Sketch your yarn bomb design.

2. Knit your design.

3. Wrap it around a tree. Tie it with a knot. It looks brighter!

These grandparents know how to have fun.

This grandad dives on wrecks.

This nana plays knights.

This gramps climbs mountains.

You can sit on this gran's knees for a story.

Holly makes apple crumble for her grandparents and step-grandparents. She has seven grandparents in her big family!